*Author:*
**John Malam** studied ancient history and
archaeology at the University of Birmingham,
England, after which he worked as an
archaeologist at the Ironbridge Gorge Museum
in Shropshire. He is now an author, specialising
in information books for children. He lives in
Cheshire with his wife and their two children.
Find out more at: www.johnmalam.co.uk

*Artist:*
**David Antram** was born in Brighton, England,
in 1958. He studied at Eastbourne College of Art
and then worked in advertising for fifteen years
before becoming a full-time artist. He has
illustrated many children's non-fiction books.

*Series creator:*
**David Salariya** was born in Dundee, Scotland.
He has illustrated a wide range of books and has
created and designed many new series for
publishers in the UK and overseas. He established
The Salariya Book Company in 1989. He lives in
Brighton with his wife, illustrator Shirley Willis,
and their son Jonathan.

*Editor:* **Tanya Kant**

*Editorial Assistant:* **Mark Williams**

Published in Great Britain in 2009 by
Book House, an imprint of
**The Salariya Book Company Ltd**
25 Marlborough Place, Brighton BN1 1UB
**www.salariya.com**
**www.book-house.co.uk**

HB ISBN-13: 978-1-906370-95-4
PB ISBN-13: 978-1-906370-96-1

# SALARIYA

1 3 5 7 9 8 6 4 2

A CIP catalogue record for this book is available
from the British Library.

Printed and bound in China.
Printed on paper from sustainable sources.

# Avoid being a Skyscraper Builder!

Written by
## John Malam

Illustrated by
## David Antram

Created and designed by
## David Salariya

# The Danger Zone

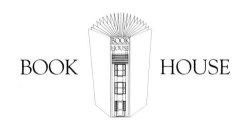

BOOK HOUSE

# Contents

# Introduction

How much worse can it get? Like millions of other workers in the United States of America during the Great Depression, you're out of a job. Every day you walk the streets of New York City, looking for work. You've been doing this for months, but no matter where you go, the message is always the same: No work.

It hasn't always been this hard. Until last year, you had a job as a builder and had enough money to buy food and pay the bills. But then came 'Black Tuesday' – 29 October 1929. It was a day of panic in the business world, and within hours companies had lost millions of dollars. Unable to pay workers' wages, these companies had to lay off (sack) many people. It was the start of the Great Depression – a time of poverty and hardship.

You lost your job, but that doesn't mean you're a loser! You've heard about a project to build a huge new skyscraper in Manhattan, one of the wealthiest parts of New York City. Stay positive, and maybe you'll find work there.

# Sky high!

# New York City rises

The island of Manhattan is the heart of New York City. It's packed with shops, hotels and offices, and has become so crowded that new buildings have to grow upwards rather than out. It's no wonder that New York is the birthplace of the skyscraper. By the end of the 1920s there are fifteen towers more than 152.5 metres (500 feet) high. But while the city is growing, your life has fallen apart. You've been out of work since Black Tuesday, and you're one of 6,000 unemployed people scraping a living on the streets of New York.

## Boom and bust

BOOM. Before the Depression, there was plenty of work for everyone. When one building job was finished, you moved on to the next. Life was good.

1929: BLACK TUESDAY. Fortunes were lost as businessmen traded at bargain prices.

BUST. The firm you worked for went out of business. You are now one of millions out of work.

1913: Woolworth Building. 60 storeys, 241 m (792 ft)

1908: Singer Building. 47 storeys, 187 m (613 ft)

1909: Metropolitan Life Insurance Tower. 50 storeys, 213 m (700 ft)

1894: Manhattan Life Insurance Building. 17 storeys, 106 m (348 ft)

Handy hint

Ask around – other men might know where there's work to be found.

1846: Trinity Church. 86 m (281 ft)

1875: New York Tribune Building. 9 storeys, 79 m (260 ft)

1902: Flatiron Building. 22 storeys, 87 m (285 ft)

1890: New York World Building. 18 storeys, 94 m (309 ft)

1889: Tower Building. 11 storeys, 49 m (160 ft)

Note: Buildings are not shown in their actual locations.

7

# Wrecker! It's your job

**A**fter selling apples on the street for a few weeks, your luck has changed. You've got a job as a wrecker on a demolition site. It's dangerous work, but the pay is good: a dollar an hour. The site is at the corner of 5th Avenue and 34th Street, where 600 workers are demolishing the Waldorf-Astoria Hotel to make way for a new skyscraper. By February 1930 your job is done. About 13,600 tonnes of iron and steel are trucked away to be recycled, and thousands of tonnes of rubble are dumped at sea.

## Dangers of demolition

*Going, going, gone!*

**HIGH-CLASS HOTEL.** Opened in 1897, the Waldorf-Astoria was New York's grandest hotel. It had more than 1,000 rooms.

**AUCTION SALE.** When the hotel closed, the contents were sold.

**FIREWOOD.** Scrap wood from the demolition of the hotel is left for the poor to take.

*This is high-class firewood!*

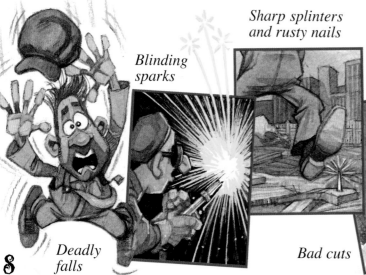

*Blinding sparks*

*Sharp splinters and rusty nails*

*Falling debris*

*Thunk!*

*Deadly falls*

*Bad cuts*

# It's a blast!

STEP BY STEP. Sticks of dynamite are pushed into holes drilled in the rock. Wires join the explosives. Iron covers laid over the holes stop debris flying out.

# Kaboom! Blasters at work

W ith the old hotel out of the way, it's time to dig the foundation pit for the new skyscraper. You join a team of blasters whose job is to dig down to solid rock. The quickest way to clear the loose soil and rock is to blow them up. You operate a bone-shaking drill. It's so loud that it damages your hearing.* This could be a problem – if you can't hear the warning whistle, you might get caught in the blast! Time is precious, and you're soon back in the pit, drilling the hole for the next ground-splitting explosion. As you blast your way across the site, earth-moving machines follow you, shifting the rubble away.

*\* Ear defenders have been invented, but most workers at this time don't like to wear them.*

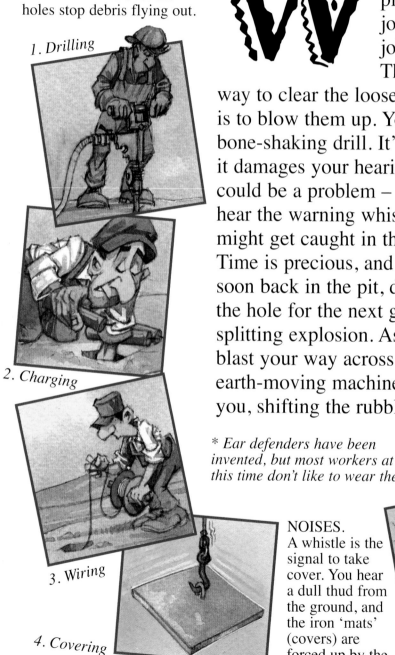

*1. Drilling*

*2. Charging*

*3. Wiring*

*4. Covering*

## Danger zone!

FATAL ACCIDENT. One man is killed when he runs into the blast area and is caught in the explosion.

NOISES. A whistle is the signal to take cover. You hear a dull thud from the ground, and the iron 'mats' (covers) are forced up by the explosion.

*5. Warning*

*6. THUD!*

# Rock bottom! Deep hole

The skyscraper is to be called the Empire State Building,* and it must be ready by May 1931. In less than eighteen months, the world's tallest building will stand where you are now! On days when there's no blasting in the foundation pit, you work as a ground man, guiding the huge bucket of a steam shovel as it clears rubble. Be careful: don't get crushed by falling rocks! After digging deep and clearing away all the debris, you find what you want – solid bedrock. Now that you've hit 'rock bottom', it's time to start raising the tower.

* 'Empire State' is a nickname for the state of New York.

## Night and day

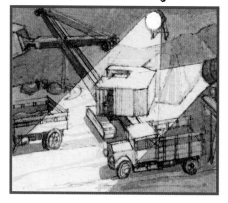

NON-STOP. The foundation pit is dug 12 m (40 ft) into the ground. Work goes on through the night.

SHOVELS. Four steam shovels scoop up the loose rock. Each shovel has three men to work it.

CRANES. Three steam cranes haul the building material and equipment into and out of the pit.

Handy hint

Don't say no to night work, or your job might be given to someone else.

splat!

Did I drop something?

DERRICKS. Stiff-leg derricks stretch to places other cranes can't reach. Three of them are on site.

TRUCKS. By March 1930, 28,529 truckloads of debris have been carried away from the site.

# Bare bones!

Help! I'm in the sticky stuff!

Grab my hand!

# A steel skeleton

t's Monday, 17 March 1930, and the first pieces of the skyscraper's steel skeleton are brought in from Pittsburgh, 388 miles (624 km) from New York City. The furnaces in America's steel city have been working flat out to make the steel beams needed. When they arrive, the beams are still warm. Each beam is numbered, and the derricks lower them into matching pier holes. Tonnes of concrete are poured into the holes, and as it sets solid, the beams are locked into the bedrock. Be careful – with metal, holes and concrete everywhere, accidents can easily happen.

## Grand designs

ALL CHANGE. The Empire State Building has been designed by architects Shreve and Lamb, who've changed their design for the tower several times.

*1928. The first design is for a tower with 50 storeys.*

# Your working day

## Handy hint

Work fast! With so much steel coming in, there's not a minute to lose.

START. Be on site by 3:30am. The steel arrives at dawn each day, and you have to start work as soon as it's unloaded.

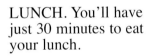

*Talk about fast food!*

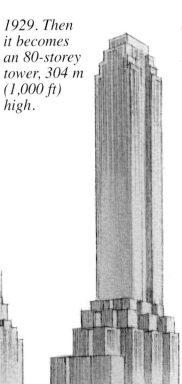

FINISH. After a 13-hour day, you'll finish at 4:30pm.

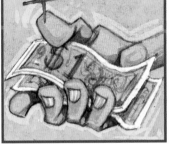

PAY. For a full day's work you'll be paid about $26 – that's $2 per hour.

LUNCH. You'll have just 30 minutes to eat your lunch.

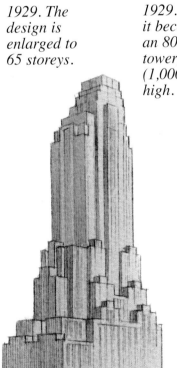

*1929. The design is enlarged to 65 storeys.*

*1929. Then it becomes an 80-storey tower, 304 m (1,000 ft) high.*

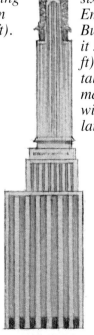

*Across town, the Chrysler Building is towering to 319 m (1,048 ft).*

*1929. Not to be outdone, the architects add six storeys to the Empire State Building, making it 320 m (1,050 ft) – the world's tallest tower. (A mast at the top will be added later.)*

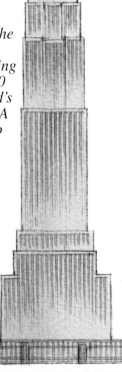

15

# Get up! Going to work

Arrghh!!

The tower rises at an incredible speed – four and a half storeys every week! It's been planned in so much detail that it's like building a jigsaw puzzle, with every beam slotting into its rightful place. The higher it rises, the higher you have to go to work. Workers on other skyscrapers have a tiring time climbing steps and ladders. But it's different on the Empire State Building. There are several lifts, some of them saved from the old Waldorf-Astoria Hotel, and you travel to work quickly and easily. But be sure you don't fall down an open lift shaft – it's a long way to the bottom.

## Danger zone!

FATAL ACCIDENT. During the building of the steel frame, one man loses his life when he falls down a lift shaft.

## How many men?

WORKFORCE. Thousands of men work on the tower. The greatest number working at any one time is 3,439, on Thursday, 14 August 1930.

Carpenter

Steel man

Plumber

Cook

Electrician

Bricklayer

Water boy

16

17

# Catch! Joining the beams

This is a noisy site. Most noise comes from the riveters – workers who join steel beams together with rivets. You're a catcher in one of the forty riveting gangs, and on a good day your team can fix 500 rivets, for which you'll earn $1.92 an hour. You have to concentrate on this job. Not only have you got to catch red-hot rivets flung to you by the furnaceman, but you've got to get them to the bucker-up man before they cool and become too hard to shape. The gunman's air gun bashes each rivet twice a second to flatten its head. The noise is enough to make you deaf, and it probably will.

Watch where you're throwing that thing!

Did I tell you about my time as a catcher?

Yes. It was riveting.

18

# How to rivet a beam

1. THE FURNACEMAN heats a rivet – a short, strong steel rod – until it's soft enough to be hammered into shape.

2. HE FLICKS the red-hot rivet to the catcher.

## Handy hint

Ouch!

Don't get burned. The rivets are red-hot, so remember to wear strong gloves.

3. THE CATCHER catches the rivet in a tin bucket.

4. HE PLACES the rivet in a hole drilled through two beams.

## Danger zone!

FATAL ACCIDENT. A swinging hoist hits a man and kills him.

ON 15 SEPTEMBER 1930 the steelwork is finished to the 86th floor. The flag is raised in a ceremony known as 'topping out'.

5. THE BUCKER-UP MAN holds the rivet in place.

6. THE GUNMAN hammers the rivet with a jackhammer. This makes the head of the rivet swell so it can't fall out of its hole.

19

# Sky boy! A good head for heights

As the tower rises, crowds gaze up from the streets far below. They watch in amazement as you walk along the narrow beams and climb up and down steel cables. Is it any wonder they call you a 'sky boy'? Of all the skywalkers working on the Empire State Building, the bravest are the Mohawk ironworkers – Native Americans with nerves of steel and seemingly no fear of heights. They make it look so easy, but it's dangerous work. One slip is all it needs for you to take the fast way down. But no sky boy has ever fallen off the tower – let's keep it that way, OK?

He'd better start flapping.

Yikes! That was my best cap!

# For the record

SMILE, PLEASE. A famous photographer has been hired to photograph the workers as they go about their jobs. If Mr Lewis Hine points his camera at you, keep still while he takes your photograph.

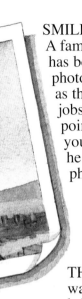

## Handy hint

When you're on a beam, don't look down. Just look to the end of the beam and keep walking. That way you'll keep your balance.

# Food and drink

THIRSTY WORK. You can have as much water as you like – just ask a water boy to bring some to you. Don't stop work.

LUNCHTIME. Listen for the whistle at midday – your 30-minute lunch break starts now.

Fweet!!

EAT OUT. If you don't want a hot meal, buy sandwiches and coffee and enjoy the view.

What's in yours?

EAT IN. For 40 cents you can have a hot meal and a slice of pie in an on-site cafe.

21

# The hard stuff!

A s soon as the steel for a new storey is in place, teams of workers start on the floors, walls and windows. After your scary work as a sky boy you thought anything would be safer – but think again. As a bricklayer you've got to lay bricks for the tower's outer walls. Each storey needs about 100,000 bricks, and they've got to be laid in a day. You work on the outside of the building, from a wooden platform called a 'duck-walk'. There's danger all around, from falling objects, weak handrails and loose bricks.

## Building materials

STONE. The outside of the building is covered with a skin of smooth limestone, brought from a quary in Indiana, 1,300 km (800 miles) away.

WINDOWS. The tower has 6,400 windows. All the window frames are painted a deep red colour on the outside.

BRICKS. Ten million bricks are used to build the walls. Trucks tip tonnes of new bricks into hoppers, and the bricks slide down into dump cars. The cars are hoisted up to the bricklayers.

# Danger zone!

FATAL ACCIDENT. A worker who fell off a duck-walk has plunged to his death.

# Weather warning!

ITS NOT JUST man-made dangers you have to worry about – nature can also cause problems.

WIND. It's far too dangerous to climb about on the steel beams in windy weather.

# World's tallest tower!

n 11 December 1929 you hear some breaking news. The entire workforce is talking about the tower's new height. Instead of stopping at 320 metres (1,050 feet), the skyscraper's final height will be 381 metres (1,250 feet). The final 61 metres (200 feet) will be a mast to which airships can be tethered. These are the aircraft of the future, and passengers will be able to fly to and from the very heart of New York City. It'll take just seven minutes to travel by lift from street level to an airship. Meanwhile, you must hold your nerve as the last steel beams are placed to make the airship mast.

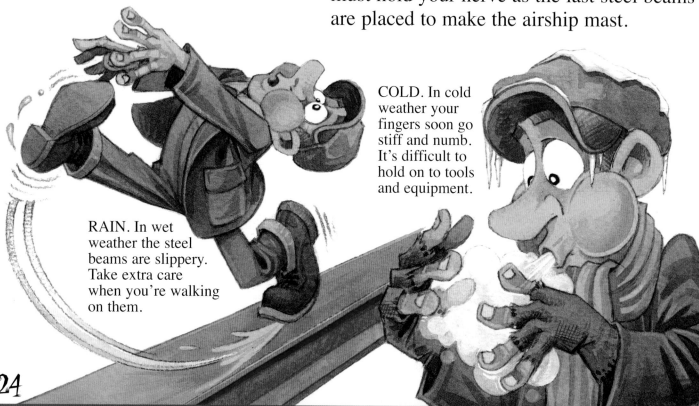

RAIN. In wet weather the steel beams are slippery. Take extra care when you're walking on them.

COLD. In cold weather your fingers soon go stiff and numb. It's difficult to hold on to tools and equipment.

Airship mooring mast

I wonder how long it would take to hit the ground from here? *

# Handy hint

Plan ahead for whatever the weather will be. Check the weather reports in each day's newspaper.

Airship

GOLDEN RIVET. To mark the placing of the final beam, Al Smith, president of the construction company, drives the last rivet home. It's made from solid gold.

I marvel at these steelworkers.*

* If there was no wind resistance, a man falling from 381 m (1,250 ft) would reach the ground in about 11 seconds.

* Al Smith's actual words.

# Sparks fly!

The walls, floors and windows are in place. Now it's time to turn the tower into a superb office block. Carpenters, plasterers, plumbers and electricians move in to flesh out the building's empty insides. As they work, there's an increased fire risk from all the flammable materials. Watchmen tour the building regularly, checking for signs of fire. Be careful around those miles of electrical cables – you wouldn't want to go down in history as the man who set fire to the Empire State Building!

## Fire!

NOVEMBER 1930. At about 6:00am, a small fire breaks out in a lunch room on the 47th floor. The fire department soon put it out.

## Finishing materials

PLASTER. Bare walls are covered with a smooth layer of plaster.

WOOD. Carpenters fit doors, panels and skirting boards in place.

MARBLE. Coloured marble from France, Germany, Belgium and Italy decorates the entrance lobby.

# Danger zone!

FATAL ACCIDENT.
A carpenter has lost his life.
He was hit by one of the
small trucks
used to move
materials
around the site.

## Handy hint

Keep your head
down. You might
get an electric
shock if you touch
one of the bare
wires hanging
from the
ceiling.

Keep away from that wire!

Too late!

Zzzzap!!

# Job done!

**Y**ou've risked your life on the world's tallest building, and after one year and 45 days, the job is done. The tower was meant to be finished by May 1931, but you, and thousands of others, have worked flat-out and finished the skyscraper in April – a whole month ahead of schedule. The building will open for business on 1 May. You can hold your head high, knowing that your hard work has paid off.

*Did I really build that?*

## How bad is bad?

NO WORK. As the Great Depression bites deeper, it's even harder to find work. By 1931, there are 50 per cent fewer building jobs in New York City than last year.

# What now?

But what's next? Once again you're out of work. Building jobs in the city are scarcer than ever, and as unemployment rises, there are more men looking for work. You have no choice but to accept handouts from the government. Without them, you'd starve. Even the Empire State Building itself is in trouble. By opening day, only 23 per cent of the offices have been rented out, and plans to tie airships to the mast have been abandoned. The Great Depression isn't over yet.

*EMPIRE STATE
BUILDING
AT A GLANCE*

*Start: March 1930
Finish: April 1931
Build time: 410 days
Height: 381 metres
  (1,250 feet)
Cost:  $24,718,000
Floors: 103
Steps: 1,860
Windows: 6,400
Workers: About 3,400
Weight: 330,000 tonnes
Fatalities: 6
Time capsule: Hidden
in the cornerstone*

*The Empire State
Building remained the
world's tallest building
until 1972.*

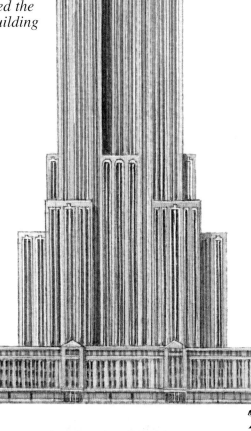

RELIEF LINE. You'll have to live off unemployment relief – money from the government.

ACROSS AMERICA, about one sixth of all American workers are out of work – around 8 million people in total.

BREAD LINE. When your unemployment money runs out, stand in line with the poor for your daily hand-out of food.

# Glossary

**Air gun** A hammer powered by compressed air; also called a jackhammer.

**Airship** A type of aircraft filled with a lighter-than-air gas. It looks like a long, thin balloon.

**Bedrock** The solid rock that lies underneath loose soil.

**Black Tuesday** 29 October 1929. On this day the stock market crashed in the United States, wiping millions of dollars off the value of companies.

**Blaster** A person who works with explosives.

**Bread line** A queue of unemployed people waiting to be given free food.

**Bucker-up man** In a riveting gang, the man who held the rivet steady with an iron bar while it was hammered by the gunman.

**Catcher** In a riveting gang, the man who caught a rivet thrown to him by the furnaceman.

**Concrete** A mixture of cement, sand and gravel that sets into a hard-wearing, solid material.

**Debris** Loose rock or rubble.

**Derrick** A crane with a long reach.

**Duck-walk** A temporary walkway made from planks of wood.

**Dynamite** A type of explosive.

**Flammable** Liable to catch fire.

**Furnaceman** In a riveting gang, the man who heated a rivet until it was red-hot, making it soft enough to hammer into shape.

**Great Depression** A time in the late 1920s and much of the 1930s when many people in America, and other countries, were out of work.

**Ground man** One of the men who worked in a steam shovel team. He guided the bucket or shovel to the right place on the ground.

**Gunman** In a riveting gang, the man who used an air gun, or jackhammer, to flatten the head of a rivet in order to join two pieces of steel together.

**Hopper** A funnel-shaped container.

**Jackhammer** Another name for an air gun.

**Marble** A type of stone that can be polished to make hard-wearing walls and floors.

**Pier** A pillar or column.

**Relief line** A queue of unemployed people waiting to be given relief, which was money paid to them by the government.

**Rivet** A short metal rod used to fix one piece of metal to another. The ends of the rivet are hammered until they swell. This prevents it from falling out of its hole.

**Sky boy** A nickname for a man who worked at great heights during the building of a skyscraper.

**Skyscraper** A very tall building.

**Steam crane** A machine powered by steam that raises and lowers heavy objects.

**Steam shovel** A machine powered by steam that digs or shovels loose ground.

**Storey** One floor of a building.

**Tongs** A tool used to hold something that is dangerous to hold in the hand, such as a hot rivet.

**Topping out** A ceremony held by builders to mark the completion of the highest point of a new building.

**Watchman** A workman who watches out for problems, especially fires.

**Water boy** A young man who carried drinking water to the workmen, and sprinkled water onto the floors to settle the dust.

**Wrecker** A person whose job is to demolish (pull down) a building.

# Index